THE
Old Photographs
SERIES

ILFORD

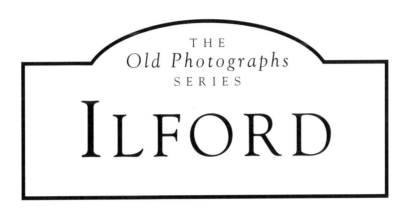

THE
Old Photographs
SERIES

ILFORD

Compiled by
Ian Dowling and Nick Harris

Redbridge
LIBRARIES

**ALAN
SUTTON**
BATH • AUGUSTA • RENNES

First published 1994
Copyright © Ian Dowling and Nick Harris, 1994

Alan Sutton Limited
12 Riverside Court
Bath BA2 3DZ

ISBN 0 7524 0050 9

Typesetting and origination
by Alan Sutton Limited
Printed in Great Britain

Contents

Acknowledgements

Miss G. Harrison
Wanstead Cricket Club
Mr Feasey
The Museum of Rural Life
Mr G. Weir
Mrs J. Boyle
Helen Tunley

All those involved from Redbridge Library, especially Sandra Haynes and
Christine Hopper in the Local History Library.

Introduction

Despite its incorporation into the newly formed London Borough of Redbridge in 1965, Ilford remains a distinct entity in the minds of many of its residents. While evidence of both Roman and Iron-age activity has been found, Ilford's Saxon origins are centred around Ilford Bridge and its name derives from Hile-Ford, meaning the crossing of the Hile (now called the Roding).

Ilford was listed in the eleventh-century Domesday Book as part of Barking, owned by the Abbey. Its oldest surviving building, the Hospital Chapel, dating from the twelfth century, was founded by Adeliza, Abbess of Barking, and was originally a hospital, almshouse and leper hospital.

By 1653 Ilford Village consisted of about fifty families, centred around the Broadway, while the hamlets of Barkingside and Little Heath contained a hundred families, living near to the Forest of Waltham at Hainault. This forest played an important part in Ilford's history throughout the seventeenth and eighteenth centuries. Royal Navy warships were constructed in part from Hainault forest oaks, which were also used for house-building. Land between the trees provided common pasture for livestock until much of the forest was cleared in 1851. The Fairlop Fair attracted large numbers of people from Essex and London to various sites in Hainault until the end of the nineteenth century.

Ilford's position on the Great Essex Road, the main route from London to Norwich, led to its growth as an important stop-over during the boom years of stagecoach travel and by 1832 stagecoaches passed through the village every half-hour. Inns such as the Angel and the White Horse provided a change of horses and rest for weary travellers.

The arrival of the Eastern Counties Railway in Ilford in 1839 was a catalyst for change. The expansion of London, coupled with periodic agricultural depressions from 1840 to 1890, encouraged the growth of new urban areas. The development of the Clements Estate from 1879, around Ilford Lane and the High Road, began Ilford's transition from village to town.

The developer, Archibald Cameron Corbett, was responsible for building over 3,000 houses on the Grange, Downshall and Mayfield Estates. He also financed the re-building of Ilford Station and provided land for Seven Kings and Goodmayes Parks. Peter Griggs was another important house-builder, completing over 2,000 properties. With this rapid growth, Ilford's population leapt from 7,645 in 1881 to 78,188 by 1911. Many of these new inhabitants voted for Griggs in December 1918 and he became Ilford's first M.P.. The opening of Eastern Avenue in 1925 and the improved railway service provided a further spur to development and by 1938 166,900 people lived in the town.

The local authority grew with its populace. Co-ordinated by just three parish overseers, an assistant overseer and a clerk in 1882, it achieved borough status in 1926. The new council administered an area that reached from Wanstead to Chadwell Heath and from the town centre to Hainault.

By this time Ilford had developed into predominantly a domitory town for London workers but was not without its own industry. Large firms such as Kelvin Hughes, Howards Limited, The Ilford Photographic Company and Plessey Radio and Television Company realised the attraction of the town's excellent transport network which included the River Roding. Sports and social clubs had flourished and retailers such as Marks and Spencer and Sainsburys were well established.

The photographs in this book vividly reflect one of the most rapid transformations from a rural to an urban community seen in this country. They also provide a record of the area before the modern age which has brought even more dramatic changes.

One
The Town Centre

Ilford Bridge looking east up Ilford Hill *c*.1900. This shows a mixture of old village properties and late nineteenth-century town houses. The bridge still has its eighteenth-century structure, with a widened roadway. The early nineteenth-century buildings, numbers one to three Ilford Hill, shown on the left, still survive today.

Ilford Hill looking towards the Broadway *c*.1900. The original village shops and houses are being replaced by the substantial two-storeyed town houses shown on the left.

Ilford Village c.1860. Despite this rural image of unmade roads, farm carts and weather-boarded buildings, street lighting has appeared and the village is growing.

Ilford Broadway and High Road c.1865. The village butchers was demolished in 1889 for the new White Horse Hotel, which in this view is next door in the High Road. The sign post reads 'Stratford and London'. Note the village policeman on the left.

Ilford Broadway - the junction of Ilford Hill, Cranbrook Road and the High Road *c*.1926. This is thought to show the decorations for Ilford's Charter Day, 21 October 1926, and the visit of the Duke and Duchess of York.

Ilford Broadway and Ilford Hill *c*.1946. Sankey's the builders merchants and Maison Riche Ladies Outfitters on either side of the Red Lion Pub have both long gone. The Broadway corner with Ilford Hill was rebuilt in the 1960s.

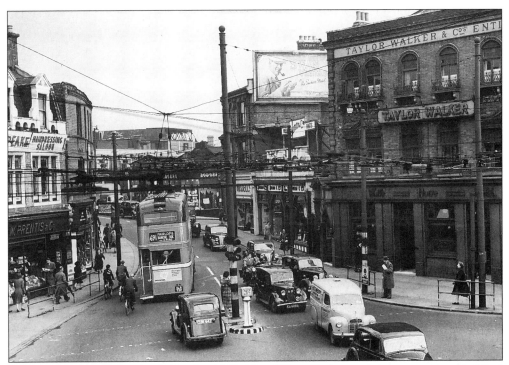

The Broadway and Cranbook Road *c*.1949. The 691 trolleybus makes its way towards Ilford Station underneath a profusion of overhead wires. The bomb-damaged Super Cinema in the distance was already closed but the building survived another eleven years.

Cranbrook Road *c*.1900. J.S. Rice the fancy drapers and its neighbour, both weather-boarded buildings, probably dated from the eighteenth century. Similar buildings could still be found in Woodford in the 1950s.

The High Road looking east from the Broadway c.1937. This view shows nearly every form of available road transport from bicycles to buses. Surprisingly, most of the buildings shown are still standing.

Outside Ilford Town Hall on the High Road, 21 October 1926. The Charter Day crowds await the departure of the Duke and Duchess of York who presented the Charter of Incorporation (the granting of Borough Status) to Ilford.

The High Road looking east towards Queens Road c.1912. The low-roofed building on the right is the Palais de Danse (Ilford Palais). This was formerly the Premier Electric Cinema but opened as the Palais in 1925.

The west side of Clements Road looking north c.1910. This site (numbers forty-two to twenty-eight) is now the home of Olympic House, Redbridge Council's offices.

Ilford Hill and the south side of the High Road c.1907. This site was cleared in March 1907 for the building of the Ilford Hippodrome which opened in 1909.

The east side of Ilford Lane c.1902. This row of shops and houses was situated on the site of the Pioneer Market. W. Butcher the Shaving Saloon and the two adjoining houses were among the oldest domestic buildings to survive into the twentieth century.

The junction of Clements Lane and Ilford Lane c.1905. The tall chimneys in the distance are part of Clements Cottages. These included the remains of the sixteenth-century farmhouse which was demolished with the cottages in 1933.

Ilford Lane looking north from Kingston Road c.1920. The shops numbered from 187 to 211 from Windsor Road to Kingston Road include Brand and Co., Estate Agents and Charles Boot, a Greengrocer.

Two
Around Ilford

The Cranbrook, 1896. This section of the brook is thought to be west of the Cranbrook Road in the fields now covered by Mansfield and Argyle Roads.

Cranbrook Road looking north from Balfour Road c.1905. The photographer has placed his cumbersome photographic equipment in the middle of the road and is obviously the centre of attention.

Cranbrook House c.1925. This development of shops and offices from sixteen to twenty-three Cranbrook Road was built in 1924.

These decorations on the Cranbrook Road are thought to be part of the Charter Day celebrations of October 1926.

Looking north along the Cranbrook Road in 1936. This is thought to show the crowds leaving Valentines Park after a cricket match.

Cranbrook Road at its junction with The Drive c.1908.

A similar view c.1928. The empty site was formerly occupied by Cranbrook Lodge, demolished in 1923. Ilford's new Telephone Exchange (VAL) is about to be constructed here replacing the 1912 building in Cleveland (now Chadwick) Road.

South Park in the 1920s. Boys looking on want to know if a skipper is wanted. 'Oh no' the girl replies, 'It's quite easy - you just have to turn the handles - that's all' (The original caption to this photograph).

The open-air swimming pool in Valentines Park in the mid-1930s. Most of the open air swimming pools in London's parks are now closed or demolished. Maintenance costs and health risks are the main reasons for their demise.

The west front of Valentines House which may have been the main entrance c.1910. The House and thirty-seven acres of grounds were bought by Ilford Council in 1907 from the Ingleby family.

Middlefield Farmyard and outbuildings c.1900. The farm was situated to the north-east and south-east of Valentines Park. The last of its fields were built over in the 1920s. The farmhouse, which was bought by Ilford Council in 1926, still stands in Perth Road.

The junction of Beehive Lane and Cranbrook Road *c.* 1925. Beehive corner has been developed with a row of shops, with Greens Stores prominent among them. In addition to owning the Greens grocery chain, Alderman Arthur Green was Chairman of King George Hospital and Managing Director of Bodgers Stores.

The same corner looking east *c*.1903. The gates on the right lead to Valentines House, home of Mrs. Clement Ingleby. The road on the left leads to the hamlet of Beehive.

Looking north along Beehive Lane towards The Beehive Pub *c*.1900. The hamlet of Beehive was still separated from Ilford town centre by open fields until Eastern Avenue opened in 1925. The name 'Beehive' came from a seventeenth century house in the vicinity.

The footpath from Wanstead Lane past Highlands Farm to Redbridge Lane, now the northern section of The Drive, in 1905.

The Drive c.1916. The southern end of The Drive was formerly the lane that led from Cranbrook Road at The Wash to Cranbrook House.

Garden City from Cranbrook Road, Ilford.

Holcombe Road *c.*1916. The northern corner of Valentines Park was developed by the Town Planning and Garden Cities Company on a twenty-acre site from 1911. The architects involved included C.M. Crickmer, Barry Parker and Raymond Unwin.

Looking east along Park Avenue from Cranbrook Road *c.*1920. The houses on the south side of Park Avenue were built in the early nineteenth century. The road was formally private with a wooden gate facing onto Cranbrook Road.

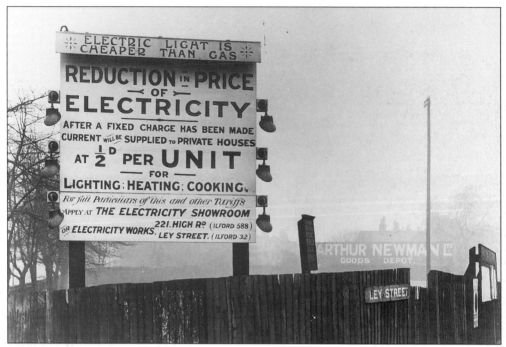

The corner of Ley Street and Cranbrook Road c.1909. This was the site of the Super Cinema and later C&A Modes. The advertisement illustrates the competition between Ilford Council Electricity department and the private Ilford Gas Company.

Balfour Road in the late 1890s.

Looking north along Hainault Street from the High Road *c*.1900. The wall on the left belongs to the gardens of Ilford Hall, a large house with grounds which was demolished soon after this picture was taken. The large lamp on the right belongs to the General Havelock Public House which had just been rebuilt.

St. Mary's Road c.1946. A group of prefabs under construction to replace houses destroyed in the Second World War. The church in the background is St. Mary's Parish Church showing the spire which has since been removed.

Three

Schooldays

Class Two at Cleveland Road Girls Board School, 1910. Mr. and Mrs. Lane were the Head Teachers of the Boys and Girls Schools respectively. The junior and infants school were opened in 1896. The three-story building was the largest erected by Ilford School Board and could accomodate 1,800 pupils.

A class at Cleveland Road Girls Board School, pre-1914. These girls had obviously been told to sit with their hands behind them while their photograph is taken.

Ilford Hall, High Road and Hainault Street *c*.1890. This large early nineteenth-century house and its grounds were formerly owned by William Hazelhurst. By 1898 it was a Girls' school run by Miss M.E. Ward. It was then used by Ilford Urban District Council for meetings until it was demolished in 1901. The site is now occupied by the shops from Boots to Hainault Street.

Ilford County High School for Girls, the victorious hockey team of 1953-54. The school, in Cranbrook Road, had been formed in the 1930s and by this time the head teacher was Miss E.B. Bull M.A.

Ilford House Academy, Ilford Hill *c*.1860. This was the site of Ilford's first school recorded by Tasker as, 'an Elizabethan house on Ilford Hill'. It may be the building shown, outside which the pupils appear to be gardening.

Outside the Super Cinema, July 1930. The Mayor of Ilford, Alderman F.D. Smith sends off 400 Ilford, Becontree and Chadwell Heath schoolboys on a council-organised holiday to Dovercourt. Councillor W.A.P. Bisson, who organised the scheme, can be seen waving on the left.

Beehive Church School, Beehive Lane *c*.1900. The 'School Strings' with teachers Ernest and Lucy Jago, whose children are included in this photograph. The school had been provided by Mrs Ingleby for children of the Valentines Estate workoers, around 1870. In 1908 it was taken over by Ilford Education Committee and renamed Valentines School. Closed in 1936-7, the buildings survived until the 1970s.

William Torbitt Junior and Infants School, Eastern Avenue and Aldborough Road c.1938. This
school was built by Ilford Education Committee, opened in 1937 and named after the pre-war
Head of Education for Ilford.

Cyclists pass Ilford College, near the junction of Alborough Road South and Benton Road c.1905.

The staff and pupils of the College (formerly 'The Pines'), in 1909 when the Headmaster was J.H. Hargreaves.

Uphall School Sports Day *c.*1910. This view looks towards buildings belonging to Howards Ltd, the chemical firm. It is thought that the sports day was held on Howards land.

Uphall School, Uphall Road in 1924. Uphall County Primary School was opened in a temporary building in 1906 but had moved into permanent buildings by 1909.

The Park Higher Grade School, Melbourne Road c.1908. This Ilford School Board building was opened in 1901. Essex County Council took it over in 1904 as a High School and the building became The Dane Secondary Modern School in 1963.

Loxford Council School, Eton Road c.1935. The boys school was opened in 1931 in a 1904 building. The First XI football team are shown here.

Goodmayes Junior School, Airthrie Road *c.*1938. The school was opened in 1909 and then reorganised in 1934. These pupils are displaying their artwork.

Class eight at Goodmayes Junior School *c.*1935.

Mayfield School, Goodmayes Lane c.1934.

First year juniors, Woodlands School, Eton Road c.1959. The former Loxford School site became Woodlands School in the 1935-6.

Woodlands Infants School c.1935.

Four
At Work

Ilford Fire Station, Oakfield Road *c.*1902. Situated behind Ilford Town Hall it was replaced by the new station in Ley Street in 1905. The fireman seated is Chief Officer John Woollard. The decorations could be celebrating the end of the Boer War in May 1902.

Ilford Fire Station, Ley Street *c.*1914. The three appliances are parked with their harnesses raised, ready to lower when the horses are brought in. Chief Officer John Woollard stands proudly by the escape ladder, firemen appear in the distance.

Ilford Fire Brigade outside the Presbyterian Church *c*.1920. The crews of both fire engines can be seen, including the driver, Mr. Charles Russell, at the left of the top row. The first engine was used to rescue people from the building while the second vehicle dealt with the blaze.

Ilford Fire Station, Ley Street *c*.1935. This is the yard at the rear of the station with the practice tower in the background. Appliance No.4 with its turntable ladder, may just have been purchased, and is going through its trials. Note the firemen's brass helmets, soon to be replaced.

Ilford Policemen on riot duty outside the Victoria Coal and Coke Co. Ltd. Colliery, Wakefield, Yorkshire September 1893. The Metropolitan Police 'K' Division includes Ilford Police Station.

Ilford Station c.1903. Ilford Council Tramcar No.10 is turning into Ley street. The Great Eastern Railway Station was opened in 1894, after being rebuilt.

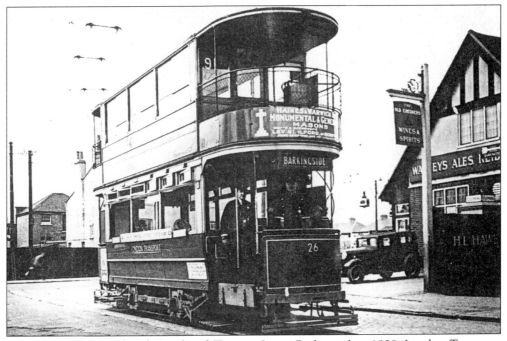

The junction of Cranbrook Road and Tanners Lane, Barkingside c.1938. London Transport tram No.26 on route ninety-one waits at the Chequers Terminus. This route was replaced by trolleybuses after 6 February 1938. This tramcar was built in 1909 for Ilford Tramways Department.

The Foundation Stone Ceremony at the King George Hospital site, Newbury Park, 5 July 1930.
The dignitaries on parade include from left to right, the Ilford Town Clerk, reading the speech;
the Lady Mayoress and Lord Mayor of London (Sir Wm. Waterlow); the Lord Lieutenant of
Essex, and on the right Ilford's Mayor, George Gunary.

The Administration and Out-patients Block of the King George Hospital, Newbury Park
c.1961. The hospital was opened on 18 July 1931 by King George and Queen Mary. The site in
Newbury Park was already occupied by Ilford Emergency Hospital which opened c.1910.
Development gradually extended over the site, rebuilding or absorbing the old hospital.

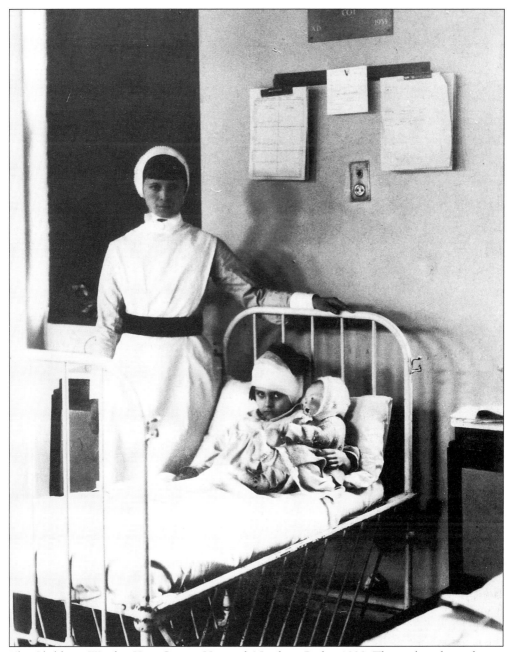

The Childrens Ward at King George Hospital, Newbury Park *c.*1933. This is thought to show a bed which had just been dedicated, hence the metal plaque on the wall. The ward itself was opened in 1927 as part of Ilford's War Memorial.

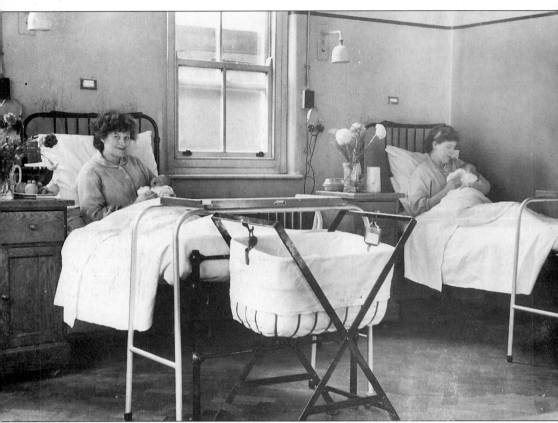

A ward at the Ilford Maternity Hospital, Newbury Park c.1952. This hospital was opened in 1926 and more recently became the West Wing of King George Hospital, housing the headquarters of the District Health Authority.

The Main Entrance of Ilford Emergency Hospital, Abbey Road c.1914. This was Ilford's only general hospital until the King George Hospital opened in 1931. The Emergency Hospital was incorporated into the new building with this entrance becoming the emergency exit for King George's. All the buildings shown here have survived although the hospital closed in 1993.

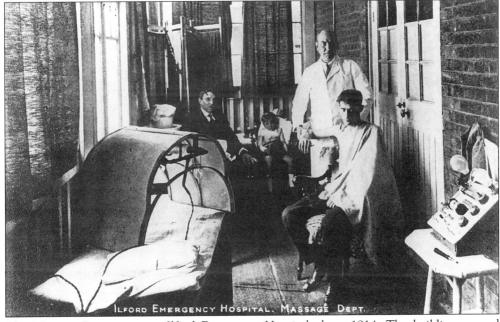

The Massage Department at Ilford Emergency Hospital also c.1914. The building opened c.1910 with 64 beds and this view reveals its 'cottage hosptial' atmosphere.

Looking north-west from Ilford Wharf on the east side of the River Roding, downstream of Ilford Bridge in 1905. The Thames Sailing Barge in the foreground is the 'Dabchick' belonging to the Eastwoods of Ilford and Barking. This barge was built in Halston in Kent in 1895 and is probably bringing in building materials.

Ilford Gasworks Wharf on the Roding by Ilford Bridge from the east bank looking north-west c.1906. The Thames Sailing Barge and the two lighters are tied up at the coaling staithe, which can be seen with a steam crane on top.

This south-west view of the Gasworks includes the late nineteenth-century gasholder, still in use nearly ninety years later.

Short Horn Dairy, Roden Street, 1887. This first modern dairy in Ilford later became Abbott's Dairies. The poster in the door window gives notice of the only meeting of the Essex Agricultural Society ever to be held in Ilford.

United Dairies (London) Ltd. Eastern Section milk float c.1930. Mr. Daniel Cook (on the right) from Grove Farm Wanstead, with his assistant, poses for the photographer.

The delivery cart of Edwin Coe's the Grocer and Greengrocer c.1930. As well as farming at Strackman's Farm, Redbridge Lane, the Coe family ran an off-licence also in Redbridge Lane at No. 53 'Coe's Corner'.

The Smithy, Beehive Lane c.1926. By this time Eastern Avenue had separated Beehive Farm (on the corner of Wanstead Lane) from the rest of the hamlet. During the 1930s the surrounding fields gradually gave way to new homes, whose owners no longer needed a smithy.

High Road from the Broadway to Clements Road *c*.1900. This shows a row of eighteenth-century buildings on the site of numbers fifty-eight to seventy-two. They include John Brewer the saddler and Walter Handley the fishmonger.

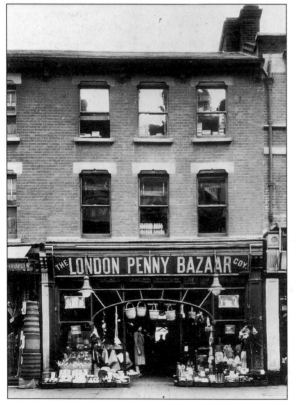

The Penny Bazaar Company, 76 High Road *c*.1920. This is the company that later changed its name to 'Marks and Spencer'. By 1939 it was the home of Jacqueens Ladies Hosiers.

John Sainsbury, butcher and provisions merchant, 14 Cranbrook Road *c*.1912. The outside display includes an eggs counter, rabbits and ducks.

A rare view showing the dairy counter in a traditional inter- war period Sainsbury's shop *c*.1928.

R.J. Moultons, General Drapers, 177-183 High Road c.1910. Moultons Stores later rebuilt these premises as a single shop, but this building was destroyed in the 1959 Harrison Gibson's fire. The rebuilt 1960s shop now houses Boots.

The warehouse goods entrance and sales offices of Harrison Gibson's 'House Furnishers and Removal Contractors' twenty-seven and twenty-nine Havelock Street 1910. The main shop in the High Road had, and still has, an entrance in Havelock Street.

The fire at Harrison Gibson's on 16 March 1959 burns fiercely, as two of the forty-two pumps and ten special appliances called to the fire, try to bring the blaze under control.

Looking east from the Town Hall along Ilford High Road on 17 March 1959 shows the effects of one of the greatest fires in Ilford since 1945. Moultons stores and Harrison Gibson stores were gutted in the blaze that may have been caused by building work.

Henry Hughes and Sons Ltd., (Later Kelvin Hughes), New North Road in Barkingside, mid 1930s. This shows a section of the shop with workers polishing lenses for optical equipment. Binoculars and telescopes made here were sold under the trade name 'Husun'.

Opposite: The chimney of Ilford Council's dust destructor works on Suffolk Road, built in 1916, is about to be come dust itself on 14 March 1957. It consisted of 600 tons of bricks and was 150 feet high.

A delivery wagon of Ilford Films Ltd. of Roden Street *c.*1904. This Thorneycroft Steam Wagon was used on Ilford's route to the Selo works in Brentwood. The driver's mate on the right is William Golding.

Staff at the Ilford Steam Sanitary Laundry Co. Ltd., Ley Street *c*.1910. This laundry was founded in 1899 and was one of many catering for the needs of the many city clerks living in the area.

Butlers Watercress beds on the banks of the Roding *c*.1895. These were situated between Uphall Road and the River near the site of Uphall Mount (Mount Road).

Five

People and Places

Ilford Town Hall, High Road *c.*1903. The Town Hall was opened in December 1901 and had cost £24,000 to build. The small entrance in Oakfield Road on the left of this view led to the Fire and Ambulance Stations.

Ilford Hippodrome, Broadway and Ilford Lane *c.*1910. Designed by Frank Matcham, this music hall was opened on 8 November 1909 at a cost of £35,000. It had seating for 2,500 people with standing room for an additional 500. The main entrance shown was at an angle to the auditorium, the rear of which was further down Ilford Lane. It was partly demolished after a V2 rocket exploded nearby on 12 January 1945 and the remains were cleared in 1957.

Ilford Central Library, Oakfield Road c.1930 The Library was opened by the Mayor Alderman Dane on 7 June 1927. It was built as an extension to the Borough's existing Town Hall.

The enquiry desk at Ilford Central Library c.1967. This library was replaced by the modern building in March 1986.

Ilford Council in session at the Town Hall, May 1930. The Mayor, Alderman H.G. Odell, standing and the Deputy Mayor, F. D. Smith to his left, are in attendance.

The first meeting of the London Borough of Redbridge Council at Ilford Town Hall in May 1964 with Cllr. H.D. Cowan in the Chair. The new Borough of Redbridge was formed in 1964/65 from the Boroughs of Ilford, Wanstead and Woodford, and parts of Chigwell.

Ilford Swimming Baths on the High
Road 18 September 1930. Near
completion in this photograph, they
finally opened on 24 January 1931.

Ilford/Cranbrook Castle in The Drive
c.1900. This mausoleum was built in
1765 by the Raymond family of
nearby Highlands Farm. It was never
used and was converted into
accommodation. The Port of London
Authority bought the site for a sports
field in 1923 and demolished the
Castle.

King George V at the opening of King George Hopsital, 18 July 1931. The King, who has just inspected the Guard of Honour mounted by the 4th Battalion of The Essex Regiment, is accompanied by Brigadier General R.B. Colvin, the Lord Lieutenant of Essex.

Valentines Park Pageant of Essex, 2-9 July 1932. This is thought to show episode five - The Siege Of Colchester - during the Civil War. The Pageants were held to raise money for the funding of the King George Hospital, which had opened a year earlier.

The Duke of Edinburgh's visit to Goodmayes Hospital, 28 October 1953. The Duke is being met by Ian McLeod M.P., Minister of Health. The gentleman standing in the middle is Mr. G. Somerville, Physician Superintendant of Goodmayes Hospital.

King George VI and Queen Elizabeth in Ley Street, 9 May 1945. The day after the end of the war in Europe, the Royal Family visited Ilford as part of a tour of London and its suburbs. The Royal couple are shown with Mrs. Beatrice Harding, Ilford's first female Mayor (1944-45). Princess Elizabeth can be seen behind her father.

Princess Elizabeth with the Mayor and Mayoress, Alderman and Mrs S.c.V. Woods, view the 1,000th council house to be completed since 1945, on 25 October 1949.

The visit of the Princess Royal to Ilford Town Hall 9 May 1950. The Princess is shown with the Mayor, Alderman S.C. Woods, and Mrs I.W. Ptolemy Nursing Superintendant of the 154th Essex Red Cross, inspecting the Red Cross Flag Day Depot.

The Duchess of York leaves the Super Cinema, 21 October 1926. The bear was a gift for Princess Elizabeth from the children of Ilford. The Mayor, Frederick Wise, and the Duke of York are also shown.

Charter Day crowd outside the Super Cinema, 21 October 1926. The policemen seem to be enjoying themselves just as much as the public on the day that Ilford became a borough.

Ilford Lodge c.1895. This is thought to show the family of Mr N. Hughes, the Steward of the Park Club which was then occupying the former 1820s country house, last owned by Mr C.H. Binney. The house was demolished in 1960, making way for a multi-story car park.

George Edward Tasker and family, October 1911. This may be the garden of eighty-four Mayfair Avenue, the family home since 1898. George Tasker was the author of 'Ilford Past and Present', the definitive book on Ilford's early history, published in 1901. He is shown with his wife Mary, sister-in-law, eldest son and youngest son (Stanley) and daughter.

Edmund John Beal, the first Chairman of Ilford Urban District Council in 1895. He was also a J.P., a County Alderman, Poor Law Guardian, and first Chairman of the Ilford Conservative Association. Until his retirement in 1893, Edmund Beal was the only Chemist in Ilford.

The garden and west facade of Cranbrook Hall from the lake *c.*1900. This building probably dated from the eighteenth century although parts were much older. The house was sold to Griggs the Developer in 1897 and demolished in 1900. The site is now divided between twelve and sixteen De Vere Gardens and five to nine Endsleigh Gardens

The River Roding near the Red Bridge, 27 October 1921. 'Beating the bounds of the parish' was a custom once observed all over England on Ascension Day. The school children, accompanied by the clergy and parish officials, walked all round the parish boundary, and at one time were beaten with willow wands or ducked in streams.

Six

Freetime

The 16th Company Boys Brigade from the High Road Baptist Church, Ilford *c.*1950.

The 16th Company Boys Brigade Football Team *c.*1949, outside the High Road Baptist Church, Ilford.

Officers of the Ilford Boys Life Brigade, at their camp in Felixstowe in 1924.

Ilford Guides *c*.1958. The Ilford division of the Girl Guides was part of the County of London Guides. The Division Commissioner in 1958/59 was Miss W.M. Price and Miss R.M. Fordman was the Divisional Secretary.

2nd Ilford Boy Scout Troop *c*.1912.

The Ilford Salvation Army Young Peoples' Band and singing company *c.*1924. The Salvation Army has been active in Ilford since 7 March 1886, when Lieutenant Willie Hunter held a meeting above Gilderson's in Cleveland Road. Within a few weeks he had recruited eighty soldiers. A flag was presented to the new corps on 22 April followed by a 'Great Camp Meeting'. Robert Gilderdson became the first treasurer of the Ilford Corps.

orter E.Peskett A.J.Spelling G.W.Webb A.Reynolds A.Davey H.Drosse J.H.Dane C.J.Norman A.Porter J.Miles W.A.White C.H.Pearce J.S.Morgan W.D.Goldi

Players and officials of Ilford Football Club *c.*1908. The club was founded in 1881 and originally played on a site now covered by Ilford Town Hall. Their first match was against Forest Gate Amateurs which they won 2-0 with a team that included Alfred Porter as captain. In 1907-8 they won the Essex Senior Cup, beating Walthamstow Grange 3-0.

Winners of the London Senior Cup - Ilford F.C., 8 May 1954. Ilford beat Hounslow Town 4-1 in the final and won the cup for the fourth time. In the same season they also won the Essex Thameside Trophy by beating Leytonstone 4-0.

Players and officials of Ilford and Wanstead Cricket Club *c*.1920.

Essex Beagles Athletic Club members *c*.1900. The club was formed in 1887 as the Beaumont Harriers but became the Essex Beagles in July 1891.

Ilford Wanderers Rugby Football Club XV c.1926. The club was founded in 1896 by F.C. Potter-Irwin and A.J. Mason. In 1926 the first seven-a-side competition to be played in England was organised by the Wanderers. Until 1980 the club played at Gordon Fields, where this photograph was taken.

Ilford Ladies Gymnastic Group *c*.1907.

The Ladies Team at Wanstead Cricket Club *c*.1890.

Circuit Tennis Club, Eastern Avenue Methodist Church in the late-1950s.

The Lord Napier, Green Lane, Goodmayes c.1910. This shows the public house before the major extensions of 1912. The brewers, Taylor Walker and Company of Limehouse, built an enlarged bar on the west side, designed by William Bradford and Son of Regent Street, London. The publican during this period was Alfred Hollingshead.

Seven

Military Matters

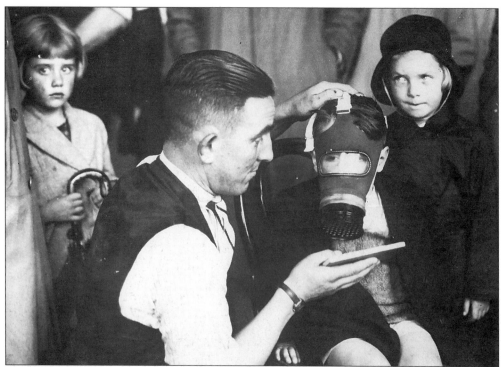

Fitting children with gas-masks at Ilford Town Hall during the Munich Crisis, September 1938.

Digging trenches in Valentines Park, 1938. The threat of the outbreak of war with Germany increased air-raid precautions.

Local Home Guard Units *c*.1942. This platoon is heavily-armed with two Vickers machine guns and at least three Browning automatic rifles. The 12th City of London (Barking and Ilford) Batalion was formed on 1 February 1941 and stood down on 1 November 1944.

The 4th Battalion of the Essex Regiment marching down Ilford High Road prior to their departure for the Western Front in 1940.

Officers from the Ilford Air Training Corps and the Royal Air Force, with Air Marshall Sir W. Mitchell *c*.1943.

Royal Flying Corps officers from the 44th squadron at Hainault Farm Airfield c.1917.

Some of the ground crew at Hainault Farm Airfield c.1917.

Ilford Fire Service c.1941. The Auxiliary Fire Service was formed in Ilford in 1938. This picture shows a section with their trailer pump on duty near Barking Creek.

Ilford Fire Brigade c.1942. The May 1941 Blitz on London prompted the Government to create the National Fire Service.

A local women's section of the National Fire Service c.1942.

Air-raid Wardens Post No. 31, Loudoun Avenue, Barkingside *c*.1942.

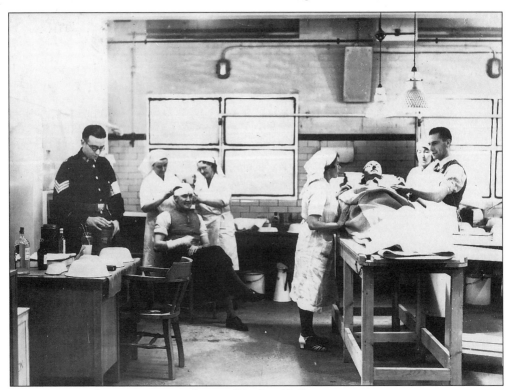

An A.R.P. casualty station, 'somewhere in Ilford', *c*.1942.

A.R.P. workers can be seen moving the wheels of a wrecked German bomber shot down in London during a raid on 24 March 1944. A total of 143 aircraft which took part in the raid, of which fifteen were shot down, including a Junkers JU88 A-4 which crashed in Redbridge Lane.

Lord Kindersley on a visit to Ilford during War Weapons Week in May 1941.

The staff of Ilford Municipal Libraries, assisted by staff of a local bookshop are sorting books during Ilford's Book Drive in 1943.

Local residents during the Blitz at the entrance to the Gants Hill tube tunnel *c.*1942. Many long nights were spent in this air-raid shelter. The tunnel was part of the pre-war extension to the Central Line from Leytonstone to Newbury Park which was suspended at the outbreak of war in 1939. Between 1940-45 the already-built tube tunnel was used as an air-raid shelter and by Plessey Ltd. for munitions production. The line was completed for use by London Underground in 1947.

Employees of Messrs H. Chappell and Co. Ltd., Chadwell Heath, can be seen 'digging for victory' on the firm's allotment, *c.*1940.

Land Army girls on a farm in Hainault *c.*1940. The Women's Land Army was first formed during the first world war, but its rebirth during 1940 led to 80,000 women working on the land by 1943.

Residents enjoying afternoon tea during wartime in Green Lane *c*.1942. The smiling faces and thumbs-up sign show the, 'we can take it' spirit. This photograph would have been passed by the censor as a morale-boosting scene.

A street scene during Ilford's victory celebrations, August 1945. The end of the Second World War was announced during a radio broadcast on Tuesday 14 August, at midnight. Wednesday and Thursday were declared Public Holidays and long queues formed at bakers and grocers while church bells rang from 7.30 in the morning.

Eight

Barkingside

The Red Bridge, with Wanstead Pumping Station in the distance c.1920. Before Eastern Avenue was opened in 1923, the route to Barkingside from Wanstead was via Wanstead Lane and Barkingside Lane (later called Cranbrook Road).

Roding Lane c.1920. The farms at Fernhall, Carswell and St. Swithins, bordering Roding Lane, survived into the 1930s. The buildings shown above were demolished in 1934.

The River Roding floods Whitney Avenue *c*.1947. The estate, which was built on the former Fernhall Farm, included Whitney Avenue was subject to periodic flooding. The Roding has since been straightened south of this site and the meander is now underneath the M11/A406 interchange.

This is Shackman's Farmhouse, which was north of Redbridge Lane, and was tenanted by the Coe family prior to its demolition in 1926.

Sitting at the wheel of the farm tractor is Eric Coe, son of George Coe, the last farmer of Shackman's Farm *c.*1920.

Washing and trimming turnips on Dunspring Farm, Barkingside c.1910. This farm was situated by Dunspring Lane between what are now Fullwell and Clayhall Avenues. In the late nineteenth and early twentieth centuries Ilford was noted for its potato and turnip fields, hence its description as 'all sky and turnips'.

Barkingside Police Station on Cranbrook Road by Mossford Green c.1905. This eighteenth-century building was originally the vicarage of Holy Trinity Church. In 1875 it had become the Mossford Arms alehouse but by 1880 it had been converted into Barkingside Police Station House, K Division. It closed down on 4 December 1961. The new building, on the same site, a station and a sub-divisional headquarters, opened for business on 7 September 1964. The tram belonging to Ilford Corporation Tramways is waiting at the terminus of route 91 by the Chequers Inn.

Barkingside High Street looking northwards *c*.1900.

Barkingside High Street *c*.1934.

Bute Road c.1914. These houses on the Hamilton estate, south of Highfields Farm, were built in 1905/6 for Messrs. Fuller and Wright of lower Edmonton and building continued in the 1920s for various developers.

The village forge, Mossford Green c.1910.

The Red House in Roding Lane South, viewed from the River Roding *c.*1914.

Gaysham Hall after being badly damaged by a V1 flying bomb on 24 June 1944. This seventeenth-century manor house was demolished in 1947 and the site is now occupied by flats in Longwood Gardens.

Road workers from Muirhead Macdonald and Wilson Ltd., constructing the Eastern Avenue c.1921. The road was officially opened by Prince Henry on 25 March 1925.

An aerial view of the Eastern Avenue from Gants Hill to Newbury Park c.1928. The new road stopped at the junction with Ley Street where the original Hatch Lane continued and crossed the railway line at Newbury Park station. This section caused traffic congestion for many more years.

The Eastern Avenue at the Gants Hill roundabout c.1928. The Savoy Cinema was opened on the empty site in the background on 3 September 1934 and the George Coles-designed building could seat 1726 people. Its first film programme included 'Queen Christina' and 'Journal of a Crime' and it became an Odeon in 1949.

Dr. Barnardo's Village Home for Girls, Barkingside *c.*1910. This complex of buildings was built between 1875-1907. The Cairns Memorial Cottage of 1887, with its clocktower, the fountain and several cottages can be seen in this view.

Dr. Thomas John Barnado, founder of The Barnardo Homes (1845-1905). Mossford House in Barkingside was leased in 1874 as the Home for Orphaned and Destitute Girls and later became the Village Home. The idea of housing girls in family groups in separate cottages was Barnardos. He died owing over £50,000, a debt which was cleared by a memorial fund.

The Duke of York visiting the Dr. Barnado's Girls' Village Homes at Barkingside on 27 June 1931 accompanied by the Mayor, Mr. H.G. Odell.

Three girls from Dr. Barnardo's Home with a basket of flowers for the Duchess of York.

The Fairlop Boat at Barkingside *c.*1900. The annual Fairlop fair was started by Daniel Day, a landowner from Wapping, in the early eighteenth century around the Fairlop Oak in Hainault Forest (the decayed Oak had blown down in 1820). By the 1840s the fair had grown to attract 200,000 people. The forest was cleared in the 1850s, but the fair continued on various sites until the late nineteenth century. The boat shown here was part of a procession which travelled from Wapping to Fairlop carrying block or pump makers, Daniel Day's original profession. The procession originates from Day's bad experiences on eighteenth-century roads. He used to travel by river to Barking, then by carriage to Fairlop.

Nine

Around Seven Kings
and Goodmayes

William Bond's Farm, Ley Street *c*.1895. Mr. Bond, a local market gardener is shown with some of his farmworkers and a cartload of cabbages bound for London.

Looking north from Perth Road along Ley Street in 1903. The buildings on the left are the just-completed Ilford Tramways car sheds. The adjacent site was developed for Ilford Fire Station and Council Depot and opened in 1905.

Looking north-east from Hainault Street along Ley Street *c*.1937. The tramlines running down the middle of the road regularly caused traffic congestion and were replaced by buses in Ilford by 1939.

All modes of transport on the High Road, Seven Kings by the bus garage *c*.1920. The tram passes between motor buses and lorries, which won the competition for road space with the tramway. The horse and cart belong to Ilford's rural past.

119

The London General Omnibus Garage, High Road, Seven Kings, which opened in 1913. Shown here are a group of drivers and conductors in August 1924.

The Seven Kings Library and Council Rates Office, High Road, Seven Kings, which opened on 17 April 1909. It is thought that the illuminations were for a coronation, possibly that of King George VI in 1936.

Seven Kings United Methodist Church School teachers c.1905. The church was opened in 1905 and enlarged in 1923. Among its leading members were A.E. Williams, secretary and biographer of Dr. Barnardo.

The Happy Valley c.1905. The Happy Valley was a wooded dell near Aldborough Road, through which Seven Kings Water flowed. When the Seven Kings Recreation Ground was built, part of the Happy Valley was included in it. It was later by crossed by the Eastern Avenue.

The High Road, Goodmayes *c.*1905 at its junction with Barley Lane. William Stearn's coffee rooms were offering a large mug of tea for 1d, hot pea soup for 1d–2d and two water buckets on the pavement for the horses.

Seven Kings Hotel on the High Road *c.*1912. A group of London General Company omnibuses are parked to the right of the site which was soon to be occupied by the new garage (see page 120).

Goodmayes Farmhouse and yard, Goodmayes Lane, September 1912. This farm survived into the 1920s by which time the buildings were surrounded by houses, Breamore Road to the north and to the west Tresco Gardens. By 1939 Goodmayes Farm was just a memory and the site is now partly covered by Goodmayes Library.

The evacuation of Goodmayes school children, September 1939. The outbreak of war set in motion the government's evacuation scheme. School children were sent in parties with teachers to safe lodgings in the country. Most Goodmayes children were sent to Suffolk, one of the areas thought to be safe from bombing. The school-party shown above is waiting on Goodmayes Station to start their journey to Suffolk.

The stone laying ceremony at the Newbury Park Methodist Church, Oaks Lane, 1933. The church was promoted by J.R. Jackson and met in 1906 in a cottage in Youngs Road. In 1910 a small church was built in Perryman's Road but this closed in 1934 with the opening of the building in Oaks Lane.

All Saints Church, Goodmayes Lane c.1914. A mission district was formed in Goodmayes in 1909, this church was consecrated in 1913 and the present parish was formed the following year.

The gate from Goodmayes Farm to Goodmayes Lane, August 1912.

A rare view of the interior of the Dick Turpin in Aldborough Hatch c.1920. Before the move into its present buildings in 1913 the pub had been housed in a 300 year-old stable block belonging to the neighbouring farm. The landlord, Mr Perkins, is shown above with a local resident enjoying a pint.

Rodney 'Gipsy' Smith (1860-1947). Smith started life in a camp in Epping forest but from 1877 he preached with William Booth in the Christian Mission, and later becoming a captain in the Salvation Army. He travelled the world and became a great Methodist evangelist.

A gipsy encampment in Hainault Forest c.1890. The clearing of the majority of the forest in 1851 deprived many forest inhabitants of its broad sweeps of turfs among oak and hornbeam trees.

Looking east along the High Road in Chadwell Heath c.1905. The police station on the near right of this view was replaced in 1970. The 1895 police lamp and its base from the old station was placed in the new building's forecourt.

The No.25A from Victoria to Chadwell Heath waits outside a public house on its route c.1918. The London General Omnibus Company's B-type bus of 1910 shown here was Londons first successfully mass-produced petrol bus.